Created by Todd M. Zimmermann
Illustrated by Teddy Lu

Copyright © 2016 Oliver & Friends, Inc.

All rights reserved. No part of this publication may be reproduced, stored in a retrieval system, or transmitted, in any form or by any means, electronic, mechanical, photocopying, recording, or otherwise, without prior written consent of Oliver & Friends, Inc.

P.O. Box 13304
Chicago, IL 60613
www.olivertheornament.com

Oliver
The Ornament™

Oliver the Ornament is a heartwarming tale of one family's cherished Christmas ornaments. The story centers on Oliver, who has been with this family since Mom and Dad's very first date. Years later, Oliver, now injured and bullied, still has the magic of Christmas in his heart. The story follows Oliver's excitement for Christmas, his heartbreak, and his determination to overcome all odds to save the day. Oliver, along with his friends, will warm your heart with his kindness, humility, and love for his family and friends. We hope the story will bring families together to tell the stories of their own ornaments and the special meaning that so many of them possess. Because after all...

Every Ornament Tells a Story™

And now here's a place for you to tell yours.

Every Ornament Tells a Story™

Now here's a place for you to tell yours

THE ORNAMENT:

THE STORY:

ENTERED COLLECTION IN:

THE ORNAMENT:

THE STORY:

ENTERED COLLECTION IN:

THE ORNAMENT:
_____

THE STORY:
_____
_____
_____
_____

ENTERED COLLECTION IN:
_____

THE ORNAMENT:
_____

THE STORY:
_____
_____
_____
_____

ENTERED COLLECTION IN:
_____

THE ORNAMENT:
_____

THE STORY:
_____
_____
_____
_____

ENTERED COLLECTION IN:
_____

THE ORNAMENT:
_____

THE STORY:
_____
_____
_____
_____

ENTERED COLLECTION IN:
_____

THE ORNAMENT:
_____

THE STORY:
_____
_____
_____
_____

ENTERED COLLECTION IN:
_____

THE ORNAMENT:
_____

THE STORY:
_____
_____
_____
_____

ENTERED COLLECTION IN:
_____

THE ORNAMENT:
_____

THE STORY:
_____
_____
_____
_____

ENTERED COLLECTION IN:
_____

THE ORNAMENT:
_____

THE STORY:
_____
_____
_____
_____

ENTERED COLLECTION IN:
_____

THE ORNAMENT:
_____

THE STORY:
_____
_____
_____
_____

ENTERED COLLECTION IN:
_____

THE ORNAMENT:
_____

THE STORY:
_____
_____
_____
_____

ENTERED COLLECTION IN:
_____

THE ORNAMENT:
_____

THE STORY:
_____
_____
_____
_____

ENTERED COLLECTION IN:
_____

THE ORNAMENT:
_____

THE STORY:
_____
_____
_____
_____

ENTERED COLLECTION IN:
_____

THE ORNAMENT:
_____

THE STORY:
_____
_____
_____
_____

ENTERED COLLECTION IN:
_____

THE ORNAMENT:
_____

THE STORY:
_____
_____
_____
_____

ENTERED COLLECTION IN:
_____

THE ORNAMENT:
_____

THE STORY:
_____
_____
_____
_____

ENTERED COLLECTION IN:
_____

THE ORNAMENT:
_____

THE STORY:
_____
_____
_____
_____

ENTERED COLLECTION IN:
_____

THE ORNAMENT: _____

THE STORY: _____
_____
_____
_____

ENTERED COLLECTION IN: _____

THE ORNAMENT: _____

THE STORY: _____
_____
_____
_____

ENTERED COLLECTION IN: _____

THE ORNAMENT:
_____

THE STORY:
_____
_____
_____
_____

ENTERED COLLECTION IN:
_____

THE ORNAMENT:
_____

THE STORY:
_____
_____
_____
_____

ENTERED COLLECTION IN:
_____

THE ORNAMENT:
_____

THE STORY:
_____
_____
_____
_____

ENTERED COLLECTION IN:
_____

THE ORNAMENT:
_____

THE STORY:
_____
_____
_____
_____

ENTERED COLLECTION IN:
_____

THE ORNAMENT:
_____

THE STORY:
_____
_____
_____
_____

ENTERED COLLECTION IN:
_____

THE ORNAMENT:
_____

THE STORY:
_____
_____
_____
_____

ENTERED COLLECTION IN:
_____

THE ORNAMENT:
_____

THE STORY:
_____
_____
_____
_____

ENTERED COLLECTION IN:
_____

THE ORNAMENT:
_____

THE STORY:
_____
_____
_____
_____

ENTERED COLLECTION IN:
_____

THE ORNAMENT:
_____

THE STORY:
_____

_____

_____

_____

ENTERED COLLECTION IN:
_____

THE ORNAMENT:
_____

THE STORY:
_____

_____

_____

_____

ENTERED COLLECTION IN:
_____

THE ORNAMENT:
_____

THE STORY:
_____
_____
_____
_____

ENTERED COLLECTION IN:
_____

THE ORNAMENT:
_____

THE STORY:
_____
_____
_____
_____

ENTERED COLLECTION IN:
_____

THE ORNAMENT:

THE STORY:

ENTERED COLLECTION IN:

THE ORNAMENT:

THE STORY:

ENTERED COLLECTION IN:

THE ORNAMENT:

THE STORY:

ENTERED COLLECTION IN:

THE ORNAMENT:

THE STORY:

ENTERED COLLECTION IN:

THE ORNAMENT:

THE STORY:

ENTERED COLLECTION IN:

THE ORNAMENT:

THE STORY:

ENTERED COLLECTION IN:

THE ORNAMENT:
_____

THE STORY:
_____
_____
_____
_____

ENTERED COLLECTION IN:
_____

THE ORNAMENT:
_____

THE STORY:
_____
_____
_____
_____

ENTERED COLLECTION IN:
_____

THE ORNAMENT:

THE STORY:

ENTERED COLLECTION IN:

THE ORNAMENT:

THE STORY:

ENTERED COLLECTION IN:

THE ORNAMENT:

THE STORY:

ENTERED COLLECTION IN:

THE ORNAMENT:

THE STORY:

ENTERED COLLECTION IN:

THE ORNAMENT:

THE STORY:

ENTERED COLLECTION IN:

THE ORNAMENT:

THE STORY:

ENTERED COLLECTION IN:

THE ORNAMENT:
_____

THE STORY:
_____
_____
_____
_____

ENTERED COLLECTION IN:
_____

THE ORNAMENT:
_____

THE STORY:
_____
_____
_____
_____

ENTERED COLLECTION IN:
_____

THE ORNAMENT:

THE STORY:

ENTERED COLLECTION IN:

THE ORNAMENT:

THE STORY:

ENTERED COLLECTION IN:

THE ORNAMENT:
_____

THE STORY:
_____
_____
_____
_____

ENTERED COLLECTION IN:
_____

THE ORNAMENT:
_____

THE STORY:
_____
_____
_____
_____

ENTERED COLLECTION IN:
_____

THE ORNAMENT:
_____

THE STORY:
_____

_____

_____

_____

ENTERED COLLECTION IN:
_____

THE ORNAMENT:
_____

THE STORY:
_____

_____

_____

_____

ENTERED COLLECTION IN:
_____

THE ORNAMENT:

THE STORY:

ENTERED COLLECTION IN:

THE ORNAMENT:

THE STORY:

ENTERED COLLECTION IN:

THE ORNAMENT:

THE STORY:

ENTERED COLLECTION IN:

THE ORNAMENT:

THE STORY:

ENTERED COLLECTION IN:

THE ORNAMENT:

THE STORY:

ENTERED COLLECTION IN:

THE ORNAMENT:

THE STORY:

ENTERED COLLECTION IN:

THE ORNAMENT:
_____

THE STORY:
_____
_____
_____
_____

ENTERED COLLECTION IN:
_____

THE ORNAMENT:
_____

THE STORY:
_____
_____
_____
_____

ENTERED COLLECTION IN:
_____

THE ORNAMENT:
_____

THE STORY:
_____
_____
_____
_____

ENTERED COLLECTION IN:
_____

THE ORNAMENT:
_____

THE STORY:
_____
_____
_____
_____

ENTERED COLLECTION IN:
_____

THE ORNAMENT:
_____

THE STORY:
_____

_____

_____

ENTERED COLLECTION IN:
_____

THE ORNAMENT:
_____

THE STORY:
_____

_____

_____

ENTERED COLLECTION IN:
_____

THE ORNAMENT:
_____

THE STORY:
_____
_____
_____
_____

ENTERED COLLECTION IN:
_____

THE ORNAMENT:
_____

THE STORY:
_____
_____
_____
_____

ENTERED COLLECTION IN:
_____

THE ORNAMENT:

THE STORY:

ENTERED COLLECTION IN:

THE ORNAMENT:

THE STORY:

ENTERED COLLECTION IN:

THE ORNAMENT:
_____

THE STORY:
_____
_____
_____
_____

ENTERED COLLECTION IN:
_____

THE ORNAMENT:
_____

THE STORY:
_____
_____
_____
_____

ENTERED COLLECTION IN:
_____

Christmas Memories

(A place to remember your own special Christmas traditions)